Antoine Predock

architect 2

Antoine Predock architect 2

edited by Brad Collins and Elizabeth Zimmermann

RIZZOLI

First published in the United States of America in 1998 by
Rizzoli International Publications, Inc.
300 Park Avenue South, New York, New York 10010

ISBN 0-8478-2138-2 (hardcover) – ISBN 0-8478-2139-0 (paperback)
LC 98-67849

Cover Image: Spencer Theater, Ruidoso, New Mexico
Photograph © Timothy Hursley

Design and Composition by
    Group **C** Inc Boston/New Haven (BC, NJ, EZ)

Printed and bound in Singapore

for my mother and father

Solstice Wall   Barton Pressor '94

The Ride 8

Contents

The Ride

Antoine Predock

The beginning is an opening, an un-expected recognition that has worked its way through layers of habit—habits of thinking, habits of behavior and cultural expectation. That point of light is the beginning. And the most difficult thing for many is to recognize it and jump on it, take a ride on it.

Subsequent development sometimes leads to the elaboration of a narrative, but half the time I simply make something I like. The narrative doesn't rule. I don't test every move against it. If it is there, it is open ended, it is malleable, like the clay of the models that I make. I can change it or scrap it or reverse it. At the end you wonder what it was that started it all—what was the beginning, the so-called inspiration. It just seems to show up, as in Garcia Lorca's notion of "duende."

Agadir

palm bay resort and congress center   agadir   morocco

At Agadir I wanted to discover the cultural as well as the geographic underpinning: the Atlantic ocean, the mountains, the dune line, and the blowing sirocco. In the collage there is a concentration of vague shapes working in concert with the water that refer to important forces and elements that act on the site, and these forces are responded to directly by the building. The High Atlas Mountains silhouetted in the distance, the river coursing through them, salt water, the sirocco, and the wind from the sea all act on the site. But I wanted more than a physical understanding of the site; I wanted to understand the place poetically, and language was an important part of that: *kamar*, the moon; Bab Magreb, the sunset gateway; *l'ma*, the water. These words resonate for me; they penetrate the culture more deeply than a translation.

The site at Agadir is naturally dramatic: a sweep of dunes rises against the Atlantic and protects the undeveloped beachfront. Behind the dunes, a linear stand of black eucalyptus trees continues for miles, founded in the aquifer of the Oed Souss. Although the dune line serves as a natural protection for the coastline, holding the sea at bay, the high wave action of that section of the Atlantic has breached this line of defense. The resulting brackish water threatens the aquifer and the trees. Ecological repair was the first impulse in engaging the building site. By lodging the building in the dune line, it acts as a dune itself, closing the breach while the calligraphic, arcing breakwater defends against the northwest wave action of the Atlantic ocean.

The *sahat*, the plaza or main square, is defined by the arcing northern enclosure. A line of water issuing from the center of the *sahat* aims toward Mecca, while its curving perimeter tracks the course of the winter sun—sunrise to sunset. Culminating in the points of solstice, the building has a notch at the high noon point. Shadows are cast by a titanium-skinned gnomon that rises from the building. Although the arc of the *sahat* tracks the movement of the sun, the building also celebrates kamar, the moon, the heart of the Islamic calendar, designated by a tower from which a flame issues.

Development, exploration, is a voracious notion. It is being a cosmic omnivore. It is a kind of benign pathology. With every project, there is an attempt to digest and consume—to find, but not entirely burn up, the right kind of fuel. On the ride there have to be quiet points of reference, pauses that allow the opportunity to appreciate, to understand—like eddies that reside in the flow of the deeper channel, each possessing a different manifestation as a river moves through space and time. To move from one eddy to another, you have to reenter the main current.

The explorations come back to a consistent impulse of mine—to encounter the subject, deeply, empathetically; to get out of my head and back to some original impulse, some original power that touches different chords rather than work that is more cerebral. The intellectual component, the rational component, is there in my work and in my life, but it is tempered and balanced by this impulse to go deeper each time.

Procession is an important component in every aspect of the building—the approach to the building and site, passage through the building, and movement within the building. The processional route from the town of Agadir climbs up and over the building; the townspeople are invited to ascend the ramps, move through the *sahat*, and descend to the beach.

The 700,000-square-foot first phase of the building, comprising a 2,000-seat auditorium, a large exhibition hall with parking below, movie theaters, and a royal salon and chamber for the king of Morocco, becomes a gateway to the city, and from the city to the ocean. The internal procession from parking continues up through towers of light, the triangular towers that flank the Mecca axis.

These explorations result in the discovery, the unearthing, of geomorphic and cultural deformations or indicators that act independently or intersect and animate one another. Agadir is an example, as is Davis [p. 84], in the same way so many of the buildings are, of really looking at the underlying strata and the history of the larger geographic and cultural environment, over not just centuries but millennia: upheavals in the land, the changing course of water, paths that people have traveled—both physical and spiritual. These all become primary indicators for architecture.

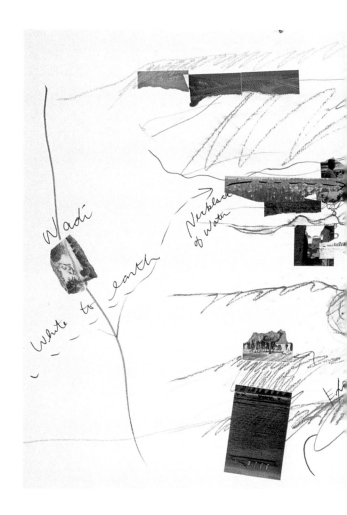

With each project, with each architectural journey, this underlying impulse to explore humanity at large and specificity of site is neither program-driven nor budget-driven. It is about creating a different conceptual foundation each time out, a foundation that grows out of an understanding of the importance of all the elements.

There are impulses that resurface in different ways in different projects, but it is not a matter of applying those to different programs. It is more a matter that the underlying discoveries lead toward certain gestures in the work that are fundamental to how people move through and around not only buildings, but different cultures in the world.

The processional sequence of the interlocking geometric watercourses that run through the site extends the Islamic garden notion of *riyadh*—linked water gardens. Black eucalyptus, palm trees, jacarandas, bougainvillaea, and night-blooming jasmine invade these watercourses. The gross assemblage is of mountainlike blocks that a finer scale hotel climbs up and over to view back toward the mountains to the east and the sea to the west.

The linked *riyadhs* culminate in the crossroads of the phase-one building. This juncture is at the main road where pedestrians, camels, mopeds, and hotel guests all funnel through Bab Mecca, the Mecca gate, before diffusing into activities: hotel check-in, event registration, shopping in the souk, or ascent up to the higher *sahat* and then on to the beach.

These are timeless impulses that get beyond the meaning "contextualism" has come to have—a word I rarely use because it has been trivialized by nostalgic readings. It has to do with a larger arena, a deeper arena. You have to spin around 360 degrees and imagine what has evolved and will evolve on the site, figure out what the platform is that is now available to ground a building on. That, for me, is context.

The predominant material of the building is sandstone, the color of the dunes—*ramla*—suggesting sand becoming stone. Inserted into that sandstone matrix are elements of concrete with marble dust aggregate of very light purplish grey, like the Mecca axis towers, and wood and metal grilles that filter light and welcome breezes off the sea. The spectrum of the traditional crafts of Morocco—metalwork, leather, ceramic tile, calligraphy, wood inlay—are revisited in a new way and used throughout the building to further anchor the project to the culture from which it derives.

cathedral church of st. john the divine   new york   new york

Considering the south transept for the Cathedral Church of St. John the Divine became a journey into developing an inner spatial understanding for taking an eclectic rehash of powerful Gothic architecture on a new ride. The cathedral is a great building, but if you have been to Chartres you realize it's a turn-of-the-century pile of stone; the true Gothic spirit didn't generate it. Its foundation is in the Eurocentrist eclecticism of American culture at the turn of the century—exactly the notion of architecture that the great battles were waged against by Louis Sullivan or Frank Lloyd Wright.

A limited, invited competition for the new south transept of the Cathedral Church of St. John the Divine in New York, the Rene Dubos Bioshelter proposes a protected environment for flora and fauna, and a refuge for man. Given the radical and experimental nature of the church's Episcopal congregation, my charge, as I saw it, was to come back and look at the building's shaky intellectual and spiritual premise and develop a principled way to look at it. Alluding to Gothic form was not an option. We needed to discover a key—a way of understanding the existing structure that could then be extrapolated to develop the south transept.

The observation of nature yields the DNA for making an architecture of divine presence. The intersection of organic geometries with the sacred numbers of the Christian tradition creates a spatial matrix from which to construct the new south transept, an inhabitable kaleidoscope of solid and void, light and shadow.

The Pantheon was a pagan temple, then it became a church; that's a rather traumatic shifting of gears. The ethos of the space changes—you can call that program—but in changing, the essential power of the space remains unaffected. In this way, buildings can exist out of time. If the south transept for St. John the Divine became a market or a bazaar, it would be a wonderful one, a kind of twenty-first-century mall. Its cosmological rootedness would remain intact because the sacred numbers that ground the scheme converge on numbers that come from the Fibonacci series, revealing the overlaps and congruencies between the sacred, the scientific, and the organic, a kind of DNA that engenders a timeless quality. The time travel that buildings can engage in, paralleling or independent of programs, is fundamental to me.

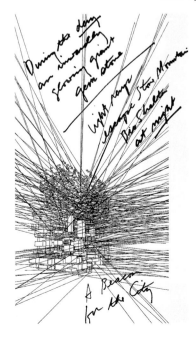

3-Dimensional Matrix (Stone Armature)

The sacred numbers determine the size and shapes of the blocks of the new stone mountain. Conceived as a solid with myriad divisions within the envelope of the transept, these numerological blocks were then "exploded," creating an interstitial realm. A spiral is then carved through this matrix along a tilted axis that aligns with the high noon summer solstice in Manhattan.

Sectionally, the spatial development starts from the rooted bedrock which metamorphoses into the stone of the building. Given the numerological proportioning, the heaviest blocks fall to the bottom while the lightest blocks at the top form the more open part of the matrix, allowing the light to enter and filter down, creating a dreamlike and sequestered sense in the lower level, musty, with the smell of censers, like a Gothic cathedral.

Cut into the bedrock at the very base of the transept is a new baptistry which utilizes a spring under the crossing of the cathedral that is currently capped. The water is released and flows on the strata of the Manhattan schist to fill the baptistry and to introduce a groundwater source into the building's passive energy system.

Architecture is a performance. It is a cat with nine lives, and those lives start with some nebulous urge. It may stop there, it may develop into the beginnings of a project, or it may develop into a completed project. Even if it is not built, like the projects in this introduction, it has a life. We do our best to play out the lives that are latent, awaiting construction, and let that become subject, rather than only the realized building becoming the subject. Then, the next idea you build. It has a life, and you talk about it afterwards, you give a lecture, you write a book—those are lives, they are all part of the performance. The reality, though, is the building riding out the ages.

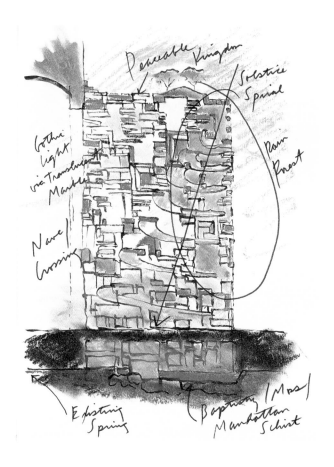

The south transept allows the ascent into the light from the crossing of the cathedral. Moving toward the light along the carved spiral ramp, chapels and gardens lodged in the stone matrix throughout the ascent give spiritual and liturgical intention to the procession, reflecting and magnifying the properties of the real world: a grape-arbored Wedding Chapel; the Chapel of the Reflecting Fish with koi floating and swimming slowly and sculpturally in a shallow pool, the light reflecting off their scales onto the limestone. Near the baptistry, the flame of the Chapel of Fire burns, invoking John the Baptist's prophesy of one who would baptize "with the holy ghost and with fire." (John 3:16)

The procession culminates, as the ramp spirals through the roof plane, in a peaceable kingdom, with plants and animals, farming and agriculture played against the Manhattan skyline. The affirmation of God's natural world, our world, informs the building of the transept and makes it the cornerstone for the beginning of a new city. It is an urban beacon which radiates light and transfigures its surroundings.

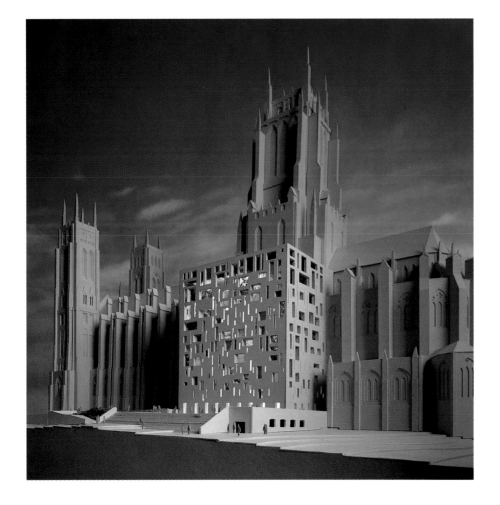

Each of the nine lives is significant. My lectures about architecture are performances. They aren't about my buildings. Buildings are about themselves. So, in a way, this book is a vast disclaimer. When you go to the Louvre, why is there a tour group in a frenzy around the Mona Lisa, listening to the guide talk about it, figuring out the right angle for their videos or photographs so they won't see their reflection in the protective Lexan? What is it that Leonardo instilled in the Mona Lisa? It has nothing to do with what the guide says, or what the photographs look like later. It is its intangible quality that has created the frenzy. Because we have seen its likeness so often, it's hard to really see it, even when we are standing there in front of it.

Atlantis
atlantis hotel and casino las vegas   nevada

When I'm at the Louvre, I beeline to the Mona Lisa; rather than look at it, I watch the behaviors associated with it. And of course, the Mona Lisa is moving me, mystically and unconsciously, as I watch the performance. This aspect of performance has much to do with architecture. The cat's nine lives that accrue around the process of making and experiencing a particular architecture are fundamental to it. But where is its deepest reality?

If we think about the performance aspect of architecture, we think of it not only as an actor but as a stage. That is something that I am aware of and act on: the building is not simply an artifact; it is a stage. In many of my buildings, such as the Dance Facility [p. 180], or the Arizona Science Center [p. 118], people physically engage them as a "ride," but there isn't a single way of moving through, there isn't a single way of encountering. It is the process of encounter that creates the building for each person. There is a physical stage and a conceptual stage—the latter made of vapor, not hard architecture.

In Las Vegas, many themes are at work: ancient Egypt, galleons locked in battle in front of a hotel, an erupting volcano, incredible light shows. They become, at best, facades, signs or names. I wanted to arrive at a systemic intention that would vibrate through the concept, as opposed to just being a facade. Plato, mystics, and clairvoyants refer to Atlantis, to its mythic presence, to embodiment in that time and that place, and I easily imagined Atlantis, through some weird plate tectonic aberration, erupting in the Nevada desert. As it erupts it evokes its cataclysmic end, as much a part of the legend as its mythic beginning. This imagined presence is like Las Vegas itself.

The project brief called for a 3,500-room hotel and 130,000-square-foot casino. Support spaces included a 1,200-seat showroom, lounges, six restaurants, 30,000 square feet of retail space, a 40,000-square-foot conference center, and parking for 4,000 cars. Instead of controlling the patron's sense of time with the typically windowless casino model, Atlantis was to be filled with light, altering one's sense of time. Where the typical casino theme stops at the gaming floor to avoid distraction, Atlantis was to be a thoroughly integrated experience—a systemic theme.

There is no facade. Instead, there is a crystalline formation that suggests inexorable growth—a curtain wall of fractured glass gently faceted and hung on the grid of the cast-in-place concrete behind. A guest gazing from the rooms through the faceted curtain wall skin would see a kaleidoscopic view of the Atlantean plateau and distant Mt. Charleston, and the imagined Death Valley beyond. The crystalline skin is fabricated with different kinds of glass— sometimes reflective, sometimes tinted, sometimes clear—depending on the solar orientation. These contrasting facets reinforce the three-dimensionality of the curtain wall.

I imagined airplanes veering off course to have a closer inspection of this Atlantean apparition emerging from the desert floor on the strip—Las Vegas Boulevard. From an aerial view, the reading is of an ice palace and of crystal— highly appropriate because crystals signify purification and are also prized by gamblers for luck.

Approaching the kinetic foreground field, slowly gesticulating monoliths are triggered by the motion of incoming patrons. Engendering a sense of expectation and, above all, optimism, the entry signals travel through time into another realm, not merely a realm of facade and one-liner narrative, but an experience that is about the integration of an idea. Rather than skinning a building with a nostalgic or bravura Las Vegas reference in front of a predictable hotel, the entire building, including the approach, is destabilized— beginning with a twenty-first-century drawbridge, raised and lowered to allow access to the spiral of the hotel.

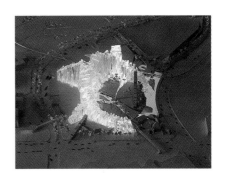

A building has as many lives as encounters: not only is a new building created as each person comes to it; each time one comes to it one creates yet another building. During a single trip a person may create more than one building. It's like walking through the wall at the Dance Facility and being open to possibility, to the potential of choreography. Of the nine lives, for me, that is the crucial life: the life of encounter with the constructed thing.

The reference to Plato's Atlantis is evident in the fragments of the subterranean culture that composes the scheme. The hotel ascends from a fractured, tectonic plateau, metamorphosing from stone and concrete into glass. Water carves its way through the plateau at the base of the hotel. From the plateau there is a journey up the spiral toward the high roller suite at the top, which, pointing north, spikes into the sky.

Choreography most often suggests the ordering of the body in space and the recording of it—a repeatable formal exercise. In that sense it is a dangerous word, a loaded word. But choreography can also be thought of, in a John Cage sense, as the recognition of a behavior in the world and seeing that behavior differently, of creating a datum or frame to understand the behavior, not out of habit but in the present moment. Architecture can be that datum or frame. It can have that kind of choreographic impulse.

This indeterminacy is more interesting to me than any kind of locked-in choreography. Even though there is an indeterminate aspect to any work of art that is repeatedly interpreted, at a deeper level indeterminacy can be a strategy rather than a response. In architecture, one can organize processional routes internally and externally, and imagine the body occupying those spaces, in somewhat expected ways, but it never turns out that way. An open-ended narrative falls into step with the open-ended choreographic intention. In my work, possibilities are provided for people to take advantage of in different ways. Encounters with buildings invite the discovery of a personal procession, the creation of a personal pattern of experience.

Indeterminacy is one end, the ongoing end, but it's not a matter simply of creating or accommodating patterns that are open-ended. Recognizing patterns is critical to my process—understanding that individual patterns of encounter are often continuations of patterns that preexist. My response to these patterns results in a matrix of intersections and trajectories, a loosely organized three-dimensional spatial matrix that isn't prescriptive—you don't have to follow it; you can short circuit it. The matrix isn't prescriptive because it isn't just physical. It is a conceptual field that includes a physical component.

At the street-level entry, waterfalls cascade from the Atlantean plateau above, flanking and framing the doors. The ascending and descending nautilus spiral is visible, tracking the sun and allowing the sun to penetrate to the pool.

Amphitheater-like gaming tiers wrap around a 60-foot-deep vortex of saltwater, which starts at the Atlantean plateau, passes through the gaming level, and drills into the earth below. Divers can access the vortex from the Atlantean plateau and are visible from the gaming area, swimming in the saltwater with fish and other sea creatures. Water-filled interstitial caves and grottos reach out from the lower depths of the vortex and connect back up to the glass sections of the floor in the gaming room, where a masked diver might appear as a gambler is pulling a slot machine handle. I can imagine Las Vegas shows in the vortex, while gamblers wander around the saltwater core, peering into it, seeing the weightless shows going on around them. The light that shimmers from the depths of the vortex implies a connection to a power source below and bathes the gaming floor in a nuclear, otherworldly glow that elevates the dark pastime of gambling to a new plateau.

Danish Archives

national archive of denmark   copenhagen   denmark

The collage for the archives tells a story that encompasses sky, geologic strata, pictographs metamorphosing into rune stones, Viking burial sites, a Viking helmet, the Gutenberg press, images from Danish movies like *Babette's Feast* and *Pelle the Conqueror,* and digital cacophony. It is a cosmic time line that includes the future and speaks to the possibilities of an archive.

An archival repository has a responsibility to its own culture and also to the world at large. Information is as old as stone tablets and papyrus—the recording of Ramses's exploits or Alexander's journeys—and as new as the latest generation of instantaneous digital storage and retrieval technology. This building is about information. Apart from our corporeal memory we have a spiritual memory and a spiritual amnesia which parallel each other— they go back forever and go on forever. This building, as in Jorge Luis Borges's *Library of Babel,* signifies infinite memory. Although acknowledging Søren Kierkegaard's understanding that poetic memory is to forget, the Danish National Archive is a fortress of memory, an accessible fortress which protects against the loss of the past, against forgetting.

Sited on the island of Amager, physically removed yet highly visible from central Copenhagen, the building is conceived of as a series of giant rune stones created by cleaving the enormous volume of the strong rooms that are required to contain physical archive material, giant stelae that contain evidence of the cultural achievements of Denmark.

I like to think of my buildings as pinball machines, advancing the participant unexpectedly from one possibility to the next, in the context of a program that has been dealt with pragmatically, but not perfunctorily. It is never "here's the front door, here's the back door, here's the most efficient route in between." My work isn't about that. It is about the possibilities of personal journeys—the trajectories that you don't take, inner journeys. If the building is successful there is an intuitive connection to the possible. It is living, open-ended choreography in an open-ended narrative

Silhouetted against the sky and the horizon, the building assumes many different forms. During the day, depending on the angle from which it is seen, there are views entirely through the building: between the heavy cores of the rune stones are glimpses of the green expanses and blue sky. At night, its character changes: light radiates out from the building between the rune stones, and the glow emanating from the surfaces of the digital runes acts as a beacon across the water to Sweden.

So, a "narrative" is not a recitation; it is an invitation to participate—a storytelling that involves the listener in the creation of the story. Architects can invent any story, there is no one out there to say the story is right or wrong. Still, architects have to satisfy the program, the practical aspects; the building has to work. But there is the timeless responsibility that transcends program because programs change—they are ephemeral.

Architects are double agents in an ongoing balancing act, balancing inner and outer worlds. Much of the discussions that surround the making of a building are about ephemera. To ignore the ephemera is an abnegation of responsibility. But to ignore the inner world, to brush over content, and give ephemera priority leaves the essential power of architecture unexplored.

The copper-composite exoskeletal skin of the building synthesizes digital media and ancient runes, collapsing time with its changeable information. With its cryptically imprinted exterior, the facet is a thirty-two-story-high by 120-foot electronic rune stone made manifest. This digital aspect is an extension of and introduction to the networks that form an unseen matrix in the building.

At the entrance, a monumental stair and a glass elevator adjacent to the information desk invite one to ascend to the archive on the second level, which opens into a space with dramatic views to the west for readers to contemplate as they wait for the retrieval of materials. Radiating from the elevator core are catwalks that connect to every strong room in the archive, minimizing the distance from one point to another. I envisioned the workers on rollerblades, turning the physical retrieval process into a dance. The central focus of the archive is the reading room, a vertical space situated in the void between the strong rooms. From the reading room, just past the service desk, there is direct access to the roof terrace with seating and views out to the verdant Amager wetlands.

Every aspect of the archive has been designed to maximize energy efficiency, including its outer surfaces, which are sheathed with copper composites of mesh and tubing that dissipate heat from the archival strong rooms. The thermal responses are very site-specific: turbines integrated into the construction harness island winds; translucent energy-generating photovoltaic sails on the roof terrace form shade structures; solar cells attached to the greenhouse provide shade and generate surplus energy that is used in the town; water from the adjacent wetlands dissipates heat build-up from the archives; rainwater is collected in cisterns on the roof surfaces to supply the building's grey water systems. The fortress of memory is a passive energy machine as well as an information machine.

This house is a kind of
excavated Rubik's Cube for a toy
designer. It presents the possibility
of many different interlocking
interior/exterior spatial
relationships within a discrete
geometric envelope.

A triangular concrete piece
sheltering a future water grotto
"slides" out of the cube and, with
its base parallel to the street,
positions the house at 45 degrees
to the street edge. The
displaced volume, the upper
terrace, becomes the crossroads of
the house.

The stucco perimeter of the cube is punctured with apertures that define moments such as the slope of a stair, or a framed view.

The lower dwelling area, located beneath the upper terrace, opens fully to the courtyard. Selective views from the upper levels to the courtyard are framed by the outer skin of the excavated cube.

The site had been occupied by a deteriorating bungalow—the only element retained was a perfect iconic 1950s kidney-shaped swimming pool.

The orientation of the house, the
perimeter walls, and the exterior
stairs and balcony create
intersecting view trajectories.
Looking west across the sloping
walls from the private aerie at the
top of the house or from the more
public deck, the view extends
over layers of neighborhoods to
the ocean.

The vertical layering of the house includes a living/kitchen zone on the ground level, an open studio on the middle level, and a private sleeping/study realm at the top. All of these areas can be accessed via separate internal and external stair systems.

Each exterior layer of the house creates a different level of privacy. The sloping walls define the main terrace at the second level and signify a private domain. The upper level balcony, which wraps above the main terrace, signifies more public and theatrical possibilities.

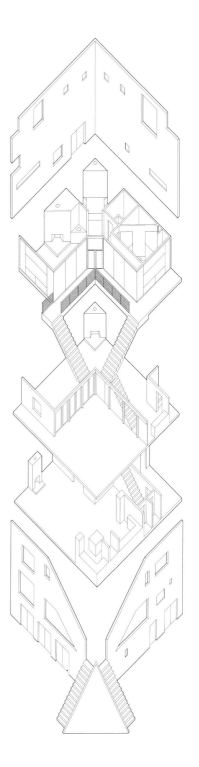

In the private aerie, sliding glass panels inside the exterior glass perimeter can render the entire southern elevation translucent or overlap to create different levels of opacity. The ability to manipulate the light environment and the view environment without resorting to drapes or blinds was very important in the spirit of this toylike house.

Centered in translucent glass walls crossed by seismic X-bracing, conventionally glazed windows look out to particularized views determined by apertures in the perimeter wall.

By manipulating the panels, a Rothko-like image is created—from a very subtle translucent green tint to a bottle green at the maximal overlap.

The glazing system of the south face on the upper level transforms the aerie into an energy-saving reflective box astride the more transparent studio level below and the more closed perimeter of the ground level. Each zone can function autonomously, or as part of the whole.

Mesa

Inserted into the conifer forest of the alpine site, the library points towards the mountain. Two elements tie the building fundamentally to the site—the first, a wedge, pierces the second, an arc.

The wedge is a place of sequestered encounter with books—intimately scaled spaces suggest cliff dwellings residing in the masonry mass. The wide open view to the mountain range via the arc signals exposure to the world.

When I was beginning to work on the scheme, I shaped it in clay—I made the clay arc, and the clay wedge. It was like a little puzzle. The wedge is about sequestered environments and escape; the arc is about view release and extroversion. Those two attitudes relate to how one encounters a book—a book can take you on two kinds of journeys: one is inward and introspective, the other far-flung and centrifugal.

The name of the mountain the library points to is Pajarito, meaning little bird. In an aerial view the library begins to look like a bird; but there was no intention to make a literal connection.

The introspective closure of the
wedge contrasts with the open
panoramic sweep of the reading
room and stacks. The radial
alignment of the stacks channels
views through the arcing glass wall
and out to the forest and mountain.

The wedge culminates in an observation deck, where it pierces the arcing section of the building, just short of its vertex.

Light slashes through an opening in
the pavilion-like metal roof over the
reading area, filtering laterally through
the apertures of the wedge and
downward through a "light canyon"
to the children's library on the
level below.

I could have focused on one possibility and made a singularly panoramic library, but it seemed important to me to have an environment that could express and allow both

experiences—internalized introspection and view release.

As the sides of the wedge converge to the north, the resulting perspectival condition draws one from the lobby across the rotunda toward the wedge's vertex, creating the main circulation route into the reading area.

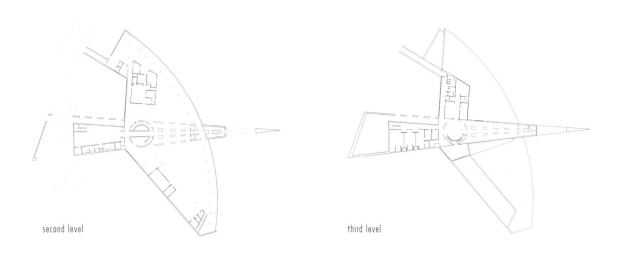

second level   third level

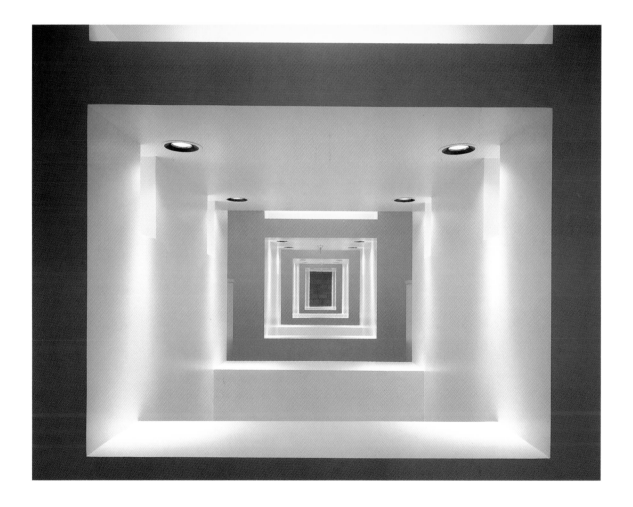

The arrival progression leads from the parking area, which is set into the trees, through a loggia to the lobby and over a bridge, which crosses the rotunda and aligns with the perspectively receding apertures in the wedge. The rotunda is inserted into the wedge and spins off a curved stair. Hugging the perimeter, the stair lands at a stepped seating/study/storytelling area, which connects to the children's library to the east and to technical services to the west.

Sectional voids bring light down to the children's library, an area of interstitial spaces carved out of the lower level of the massive masonry wedge.

The Ventura Freeway defines one edge of the site; falling away from the freeway is the tall grass and live oak biome of Southern California. It's a "Godzilla meets Bambi" site: the freeway is Godzilla, the meadow is Bambi, and the building has to mediate the two.

Though noisy, the freeway provides a great kinetic vantage point for the building. At high speed one sees the building, which houses performance spaces and the Thousand Oaks City Hall, rising out of the live oak meadow.

On the side of the fly tower, the most prominent part of the building when viewed from the freeway, is an abstract stage curtain rendered in copper. The copper panels will over time achieve an earthy patina. The stucco color of the building is the color of the dry summer grass in Southern California.

site

fifth level

third level

The building develops horizontal strata that reach out of the slope and link levels, working their way down from a high to low point.

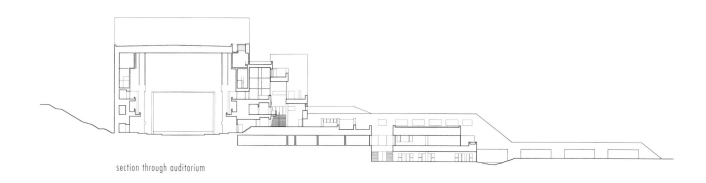

section through auditorium

The predominant arrival pattern by car is from Thousand Oaks Boulevard on the low edge of the site, where there is direct access to a parking structure.

The engagement with the site prioritizes those who work in City Hall. They can stroll out into the park, have lunch, or take a break. The terraces above are more like a public acropolis looking out over the valley. Because the grade rises from the street, there are valley views from all levels of the building, even from the ground level and the park. The park is really given to the community at large: it is accessible from Thousand Oaks Boulevard and it can be used independent of the building.

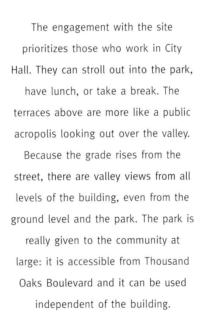

The site is assaulted by the noise of the freeway. The positioning of the building on the site with the acoustic vulnerability of a 1,800-seat performance space and a 400-seat performance space/city council chamber was problematic.

Having established a defensive wall by positioning the large-program components of the building against the freeway, the sequestered gathering terraces then fall away. On an upper terrace level a large plane of water that reflects the building, the sky, and the distant ridges also conserves energy by lending thermal stability to the spaces below.

An excavation through the building mass divides the pool from the circulation route and the terraces, and brings light down into office levels below.

Because the budget didn't provide for grand internal gathering spaces apart from the actual theater venues, abundant contiguous external spaces had to be created—the terraces, courtyards, and trellised circulation zones that are blocked by parts of the building from the freeway and the assault of the noise.

From the esplanade, the view extends across the Conejo Valley to the distant hills. One then enters the lobby, which is oriented to conduct patrons into the 1,800-seat performance space laterally rather than longitudinally. "Mini-prosceniums" define these lateral entrances—each entrance puts the audience member "on stage."

The grand stair connects all levels and provides an opportunity to view fellow patrons, as do the exterior terraces.

The sidewall of the performance space is acoustically faceted. When we were developing the large-scale model of this sidewall it seemed too highly regularized, so we dropped the model on the floor. The resultant "seismically" adjusted sidewall was then readjusted to perform acoustically.

In the auto court, one is confronted by a wall containing abstractions of a condor wing, a serpent, a starry sky. This becomes a foreground on arrival. At night, these pictograph-like images glow mysteriously from within. During the day, they illuminate the interior and serve as aberrant view ports.

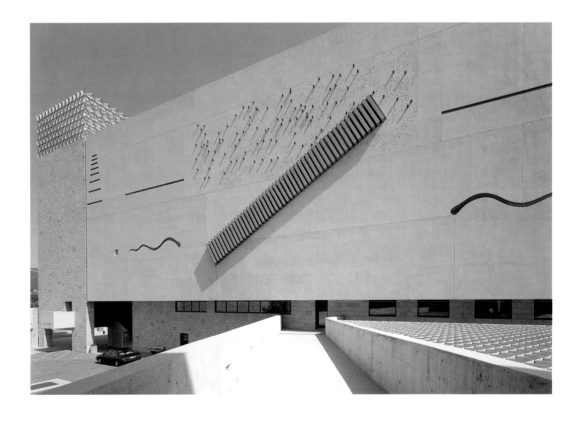

music school   university of california   santa cruz

The site for the Music School at
Santa Cruz occupies the margin of
the great meadow. The meadow is
a sacrosanct space on campus, so
the notion of building on
its edge was problematic.

The building began to develop out
of a site abstraction. It presents a
very low profile with a lone oak
tree as a pivot when viewed from
the campus behind. The campus
contains decentralized buildings
interspersed within groves of trees,
some of which occupy steeply
sloped terrain.

The music facility drifts away from
the loosely organized campus and
becomes a kind of marker
hunkering into the edge of
the meadow.

The site embraces the meadow with a high ridge of redwoods and a nearer layer of live oak trees, which ravines cut through.

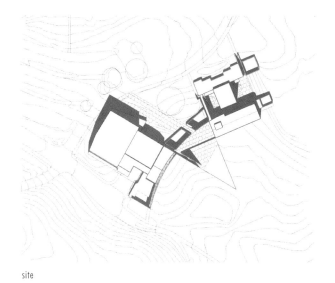

site

From the site of the building, you gaze across the meadow, across the bay to the Monterey Peninsula. The night views of the lights of Monterey twinkling and reflecting in the water are spectacular. But when the fog is in, there is only a vague sense of sky and water becoming one.

Any time, in any season, the site is a reward at the end of the journey to the building.

The recital hall is a 300-seat space of poured-in-place concrete. Its buff color alludes to the color of the meadow's dried grasses, which predominates for most of the year. The concrete block matrix reflects the meadow grass color as well.

With the recital hall as the western anchor, a split in the building opens a view across the arrival terrace to the bay beyond. The instructional spaces complete the framing of the view alignment on the building's eastern end.

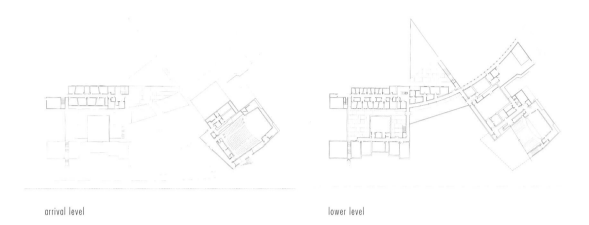

arrival level   lower level

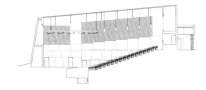

section through recital hall

In addition to the recital hall, the western building mass contains diverse rehearsal and practice spaces including a percussion studio and ensemble rehearsal space. Studios for individual instruments form a continuous linkage between western and eastern sections of the building. Music classrooms and a flexible performance space occupy the eastern section of the building.

As the site falls away from the higher entry elevation toward the meadow, the southernmost array of instructional spaces drops, with "ravines" between the southern and northern buildings. These linear courtyards provide access to instructional spaces and serve as ad hoc music practice and performance areas. The ravines form an arcing circulation route that links the eastern end of the building to the recital hall, percussion studio, and ensemble rehearsal space. An interior corridor follows the arc of the ravine, with a glass wall allowing views into a landscape of gardens and boulders.

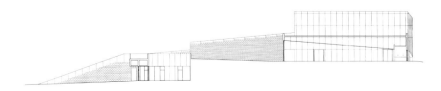

section through ravine

The cellular practice rooms have views into courtyards or toward the bay through slit windows—light control into the spaces was critical.

transverse section

longitudinal section

social sciences and humanities building   university of california davis

Flying in and out of Davis, California, the first few times, I was struck by the way watercourses carve through and deform the agricultural grid. It reminded me that topography rules, and that streams shouldn't be organized.

In my clay model an arcing line, analogous to the watercourses, carves through the orthogonal site linking the town to the student union. Rich sectional variations occur as the site is traversed from corner to corner—the building erupts from the earth through successive strata. The ground plane follows its own path as it crosses and bridges the excavated courts and passages.

The strata build vertically, creating a sectional accumulation of levels that house the various departments and overlook a subgrade network of circulation that at first seems random, but operates from the discipline of that original mark in the clay model—the curvilinear trajectory.

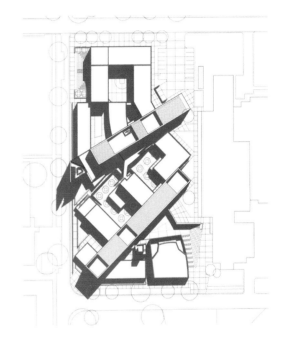

site

Out of the pile of strata rise the metal office blocks, whose ephemeral aluminum skins are associated with the sky.

The curvilinear path establishes numerous geographic identities—events that define the path or respond to it—the final purpose being that the users of the building feel as if the dozen or so departments had discrete "front doors."

The ordering system is subtle but omnipresent. In the clay model, the points along the tangent were chosen to create the proper distance and tension between the two aluminum office blocks. The blocks have slightly different sloping configurations: one culminates in a concrete stair tower and the other culminates in a library, with views in all directions.

Volumetrically, everything pulls in. When something projects, cantilevers, or bridges, it is quite a singular experience. Protrusion becomes an event.

One important aspect of the studied fragmentation of this building is that people who use it have numerous choices about the realms that they occupy. The building creates the feeling of a campus within a campus.

The partially freestanding lecture hall is lodged in the ground plane and accessed from the lower level as well as from the main campus level.

Along the path through the excavated lower level are opportunities for varied uses including seminar gatherings and social encounters. At either end are terraced seating areas.

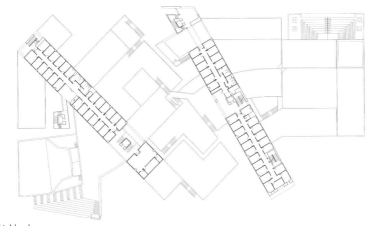

third level

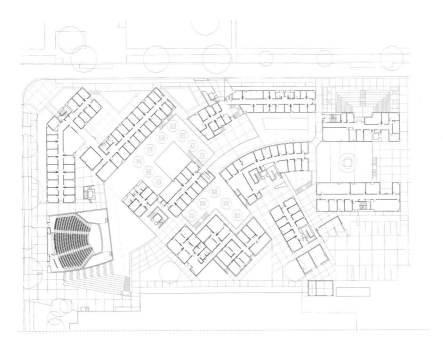

ground level

The building drops into an orthogonally grided campus, carves through it, and creates an experiential journey—giving varying geographic identities to the diverse departments.

The apertures of the building's skin are coded to articulate different kinds of internal spaces, different ways of looking out of the building, and different ways of bringing light in. Sometimes they are vertical slits on a southern exposure where light control is essential. Other times, as to the northeast, they are very open.

The Tule fog, a seasonal phenomenon in the Sacramento Valley, gathers in the interstitial spaces—eddies, courtyards, terraces, bridges—that carve through

the building. As the lower, harder-edged strata dissolve in the fog, the building is transformed and the metal blocks seem to rise out of vapor.

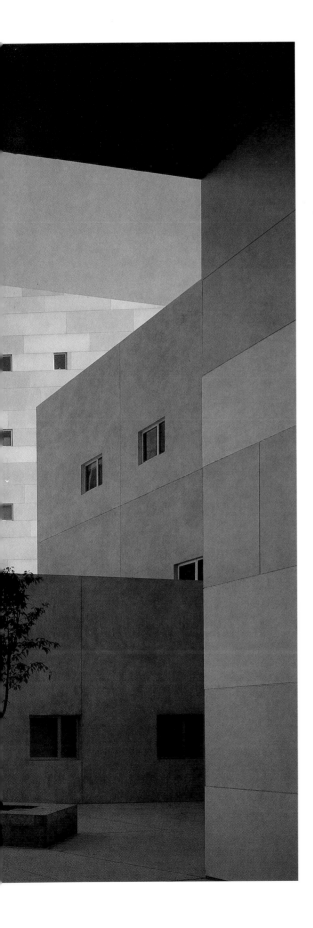

The concrete tower that terminates the end of one block allows vertical circulation and creates links between the levels, finally ascending to a kind of observatory. From that aerie, view slots follow special alignments toward distant and close range objectives.

The tower links back to the block with an open glass bridge: the glass panels don't meet—there's a gap of a half inch or so—and the floor is pierced metal, allowing the wind to whistle through the entire bridge.

All the courtyards have some relationship to agriculture in their plant materials (one courtyard is planted with tomatoes). Also, on the lower level, the surrounding agricultural realm of Davis is referenced with a grid of fruit trees.

I thought of the initial compound curve cut through the clay model as a channel, analogous to the watercourses of the Sacramento Valley. Off the "channel" are "eddies," and off these are cul-de-sacs—outdoor rooms or courtyards of varying scale, each one focusing on a departmental entry or some other event.

Areas are carved out, displaced, and excavated in the strata to form terraces and courtyards. The same is true within the metal

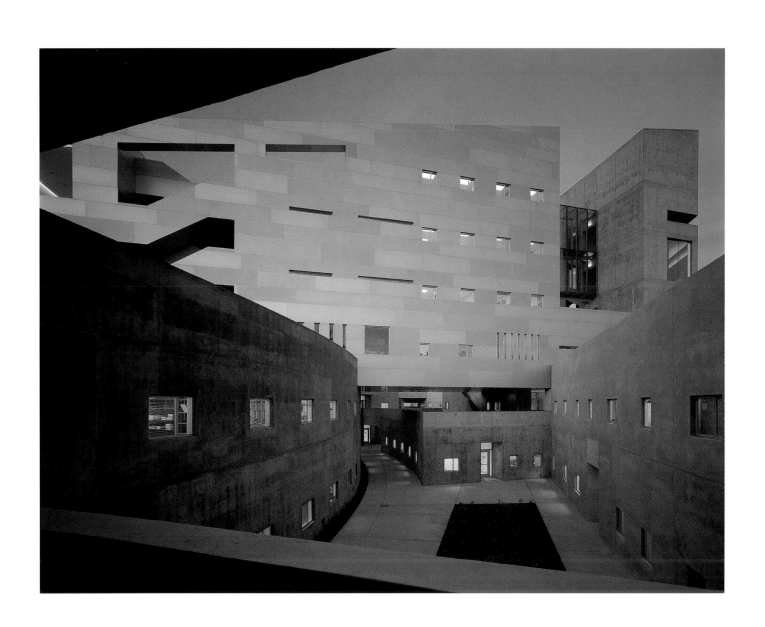

block: the incised social spaces look down into the strata below from many different vantage points.

museum of science and industry tampa florida

Although the site of the Museum of Science and Industry fronts an arterial street not far from the central downtown area, it contains a substantial acreage of wetlands, beginning with dry oak hummocks and then bay heads on the margin of the littoral zones of the water's edge—a rich habitat for wildlife. The museum, which incorporates the existing 1970s science pavillion to the east, becomes a blue and green foreground to the promise of the wetlands beyond.

The process began with a collage piece that linked images of Florida earth and sky and led to the creation of

the central information hub of the spherical theater.

The spiraling blue sphere of the Omnimax theater immediately establishes the relationship between the building and the waters of the wetlands and the Florida sky.

Cars access the museum via the split between the sphere of the Omnimax theater on the right and the lobby and main exhibition spaces on the left.

Continuing through the causeway-like arm of cast-in-place white concrete, the loop road skirts the edge of the wetlands—the building disappears for a few moments as one is lost in the forested wetlands margin. Emerging from the wetlands, one encounters the cantilevered, louvered wing that defines the entry. At this point the building appears in a new guise.

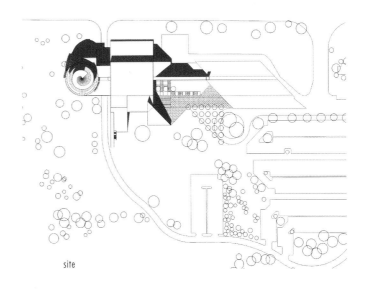

site

After parking and moving under the cantilevered wing, one enters into the gallery sequence. The piers that support the sphere spin out centrifugally from the amphitheater and form an axis which marches through the lobby and ultimately defines an outdoor dining court.

The Butterfly Pavillion is part of the entry sequence and is like a Florida

screened porch. The butterflies' wetland habitat is irrigated by a series of tanks, which are a part of a water recycling demonstration.

The ground floor lobby is surrounded
by a shop, a cafe, a branch of the
public library, temporary exhibit areas,
and assembly areas.

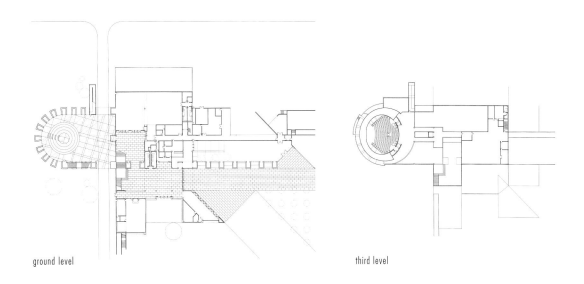

ground level   third level

A vertical slot that runs through the bridge connecting the theater with the rest of the museum, brings light to the entry roadway on the ground level and into the main exhibition spaces on the second and third floors. It also provides views of the fragmented sphere of the theater.

The concrete supports of the unraveling sphere create apertures which allow light into the amphitheater. Alignment marks scored in the concrete provide references for the sun's positions and penetration at various times of the year.

transverse section

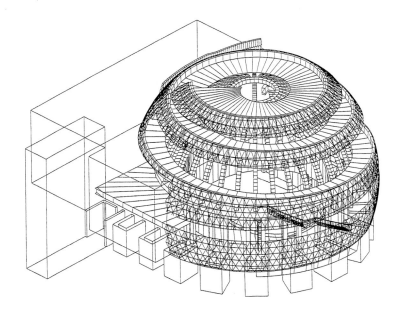

As the sphere unravels, it kaleidoscopically reflects the surrounding landscape in its shimmering blue surface, merging water with sky.

The reflective perimeter appears to peel away from the concrete inner sphere, which defines and acoustically separates the inner sanctum of the theater. The view from the spiraling ramp looks toward the city skyline. Besides being an observatory, providing views of summer storms moving across the sky, the ramp is also a venue for receptions.

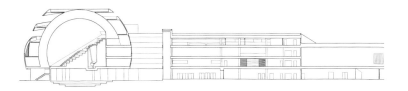

section through Omnimax theater

The porous theater screen within the sphere can be illuminated from behind so that the structural matrix that supports it becomes a prelude to the projected film images.

The collage describes an abstract journey through the land, which seemed very appropriate for a building that is a journey for children. It introduces the notion of

The project began with a collage describing the overriding site conditions of silhouette and backlight—the quality of light of the primary visitor approach from the north is very different than the intensity of the sun from the south.

The building suggests an assemblage of abstract land forms—peaks, valleys, canyons, mesas—that began to take form in the collage. The silhouette at times is devoid of detail because of the brilliance of the light from behind. An aperture in such a context can have great power.

The Center has the feeling of a citadel, somewhat enigmatic in that the inner life of the building—the hidden inner world of science—is not revealed externally. Its enigmatic presence is in contrast to central Phoenix, from which the desert has been essentially erased. The building affirms the power of the desert on a downtown site.

mirage, suggesting the ambiguity of what is ostensibly a timeless geology being phenomenologically dissolved and transformed.

The clay model follows the collage in establishing the primary organization

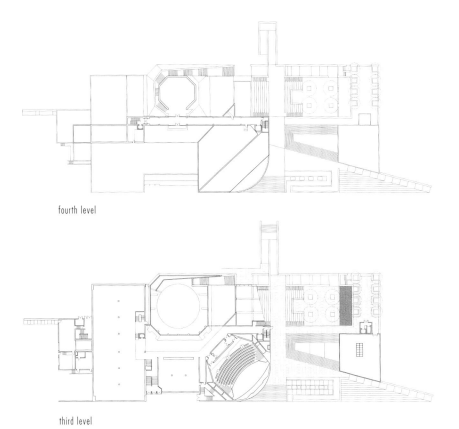

fourth level

third level

second level

The stairs follow the curved wall of the large format film theater and lead to the platform, from which the primary pieces of the building rise. This terraced apron provides access up and over the building to accomodate north-south pedestrian circulation. Urbanistically and experientially the building is a kind of permeable zone that one can climb on, descend into, and move through. In many ways, the mission of the Center—engagement, experimentation, encounter, interaction—is fulfilled by the building independent of the exhibit installations.

and silhouettes, the analogous landscape derived from the programmatic requirements.

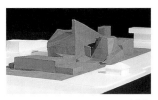

A pedestrian bridge links two city blocks; a pedestrian ramp descends below the bridge to arrive at the sunken entry court.

Stepping terraces flank an entry void leading into the lobby. From there, a procession of canyonlike spaces moves upward through the building.

Central to this experience is the bladelike metal-clad peak, intended to house celestial galleries, which, depending on the atmospheric conditions, appears to dissolve into the sky, leaving the concrete solids of the film theater and planetarium as the primary silhouette.

Procession, especially descent into and emergence out of the earth, is an essential intention.

The glass pylon focuses the approach from the north—from parking and from Heritage Square, an urban mixed use zone. The pylon is also an element in which lighting can be installed for special effects.

The trellis assembly on the raised platform offers relief from the sun, and marks an area for dining and gathering with a great view across the city to the northern mountains.

The canyonlike exhibit terrace—
surrounded by the planetarium, film
theater, "celestial peak," gallery
blocks, and passive cooling tower—
extends the connection between
interior and exterior spaces.

This aggregation, in composite,
focuses varying views of the sky and
affords protection from the elements.
These inner realms mitigate the
assault from the desert.

Flanking the volcano-like concrete mass of the planetarium, the metal-skinned blade of the "celestial peak" links exhibit halls on the west to the film theater on the east.

Carved out below the coffered concrete platforms of the pedestrian terraces and the collision of the metallic peak with anchoring landforms is the subterranean entry lobby. This sunken lobby, the gateway to the primary visitor concourse, is illuminated from a courtyard beyond to the west.

Filtered light enters the lobby through stepped eastward-oriented clerestories .

An aberrant polygonal form, juxtaposed against the orthogonal east-west alignment of the site and the main circulation route from the lobby to the exhibit halls, insinuates itself into the internal realm of the building.

This form, the envelope of the planetarium, lands in the pedestrian concourse, an area for queuing for planetarium and film showings, and also for people-watching from the overhanging balcony.

The irregular polygonal aperture,
formed by the planetarium at its apex,
floats above its base, affording views
of the city and distant landscape
through a continuous slot. More
importantly, it isolates views of the
ever changing sky. It is interesting for
children to realize that the projected
sky of the planetarium can be digitally
defined and temporally manipulated,
while the drama and variability of the
desert sky captured in the aperture
is atemporal.

The silence and detachment engendered by the inexorable movement of a

cloud, when viewed through the aperture, instills a fundamental sense of connection to the desert that contrasts with the interactive excitement of the internal exhibits.

My first encounter with the Ventana Vista site was a meeting with the client during which we mapped the site experientially. A young boy who lived nearby was playing there and showed us all the special places on the site, which was, to me, a kind of laboratory ready to receive the school. It was immediately clear that the site would be the focus—a coveted realm that would be an integral part of the educational experience. The decision was to let the desert speak for itself and operate as an ad hoc classroom.

From that encounter, walking the site and understanding the elements of the building, the basic scheme for the school was set in my mind. I then made a clay model that responded to topographic nuances by establishing a series of platforms that were generated by the site, requiring very little grading intervention. Each of those site zones became a neighborhood in a city for children.

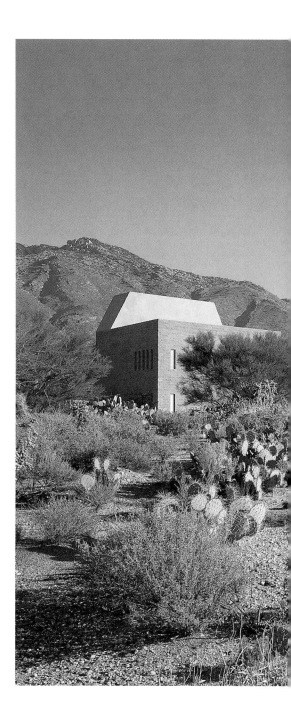

From a distance, and in silhouette, the school rides the land very specifically and precisely—its level changes follow and flow with the site.

Central to the school, a fabric tent is silhouetted against the sky and suggests the nomadic occupation of the desert, a reminder to children that life in the desert was not always sedentary or predictable.

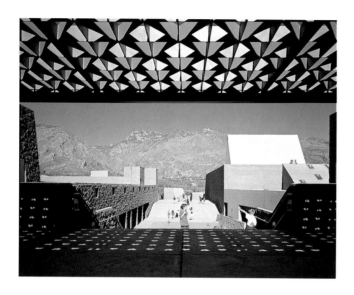

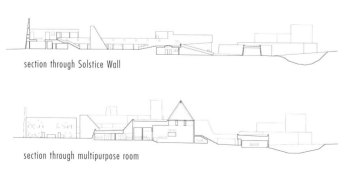

section through Solstice Wall

section through multipurpose room

Compared to the embedded, ruinlike siting of the school, the tent offers an ephemeral contrast, suggesting a transitory desert experience.

The tent also acts as an energy-saving diffuser, filtering light to the activity room below. An exterior assembly area ascends to one side of the room, allowing views down into the space through long horizontal windows.

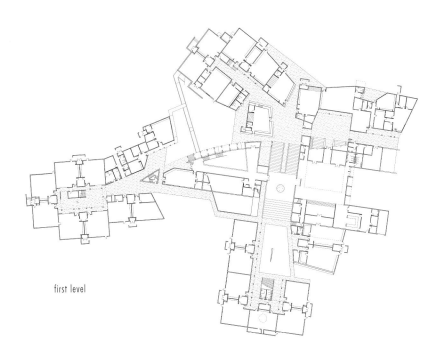

first level

The opportunity for exploration was developed out of a very tight budget by letting the buildings stake out and anchor specific areas within the site.

The incidents that occur in these areas are critical. They all focus on different forms of discovery—a vegetable garden, places for animals, spy holes in classroom walls, a solstice wall (a wall of apertures that are celestially related)—all of which create distinct atmospheric and geographic identities for each of the "neighborhoods" of the school.

One of these "neighborhoods," the fourth- and fifth-grade plateau at the highest part of the site, is reached by ascending an arcing loggia that wraps the glazed wall of the library.

Against the top of a wall in one of the highest

classrooms, a mirror set at 45 degrees functions as a periscope, revealing the panorama of the mountains.

The walls between the fourth- and fifth-grade classrooms and the courtyard are made up of large roll-up glass garage doors that allow the courtyard, depending on the time of year, to become a social and a teaching venue. The climate in the high Sonoran desert of Tucson is not so harsh as to preclude indoor-outdoor events during most of the school year.

The second- and third-grade "neighborhood" pivots around the Sorcerer's Terrace. The terrace covers a space for reading, the Desert Kaleidoscope, where kids can look into a shallow dome and up through cylindrical skylights to the sky. In a dozen or so of these apertures, desert-specific cultural artifacts, like potsherds or a kachina doll, were cast inside the acrylic skylights. By looking through to the desert sky above, or walking over and looking down, the students encounter a spectrum of desert images.

The Sorcerer's Terrace is also the
termination of the procession from
north to south. On this terrace is the
Solstice Wall. The cylinders that pierce
the wall align with the position of the
sun on specific days—such as Cinco
de Mayo or the winter solstice. The
apertures also frame specific views of
landscape and sky. The wall is both
an observatory and a beacon.

The Center for Integrated Systems, essentially a laboratory building for silicon chip and other research with adjunct office and support spaces, is a linear stone block that caps the northern end of an existing building. I imagined the building as a block of stone that covered the entire available site and was then subjected to an excavation process.

The strategy was to gently subvert the precedent established by the Richardsonian Romanesque buildings that define the central quadrangle of the Stanford campus. The Center has a knife-edged copper roof hovering over the block of stone with an inserted copper vault.

In contrast to the excavated, weighty stone block, the roof assembly appears to hover, detached and dematerialized, especially at night, when seen at a distance from the main quadrangle.

The most significant displacement from the imagined stone block occurs at the northeast corner of the building where an axial copper-lined vault is inserted, unexpectedly, into a two-story columnar, rectilinear loggia.

When viewed from the east, the copper-lined vault reads as a solid excavation; when viewed from the north, the reality of the vault as a floating object becomes clear. The tension between these two readings asserts a different interpretation from the traditional stone masonry and copper detailing of the rest of the campus.

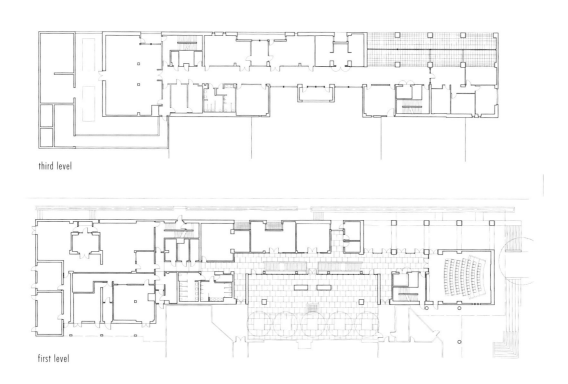

third level

first level

Under the shade of an oak, the broad steps at the east end of the building, coupled with the east-west ramp and the built-in seating of the loggia,

transform the entry sequence into a site for study and social interaction.

The loggia and vault axially project eastward toward the center of the campus, signaling entry and bringing circulation into the lobby of the building on an axis perpendicular to the central mall.

Moving beneath the vault, one senses the copper canopy lightly hovering above. The loggia functions as a sheltered continuation of the lobby and courtyard, rather than as just a circulation zone.

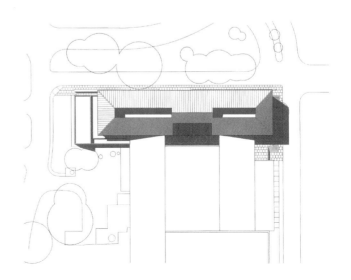

site

Suspended within the two-story-high
loggia, the copper vault is bisected at
its apex by glazing. This frees the
vault from the body of the building
and allows views north to Serra Mall.
Half of the vault spills into the interior
of the second level of the building
and the expectation of
a traditional vault type is again
reversed—rather than being
interstitially engaged and read only as
a residual volume, here the volumetric
completion of the vault is expressed.

Apertures in the stone block articulate different programmatic scales, allow light to penetrate to different degrees, and release views in different ways— intermediate scale openings allow light into faculty offices; slots bring light into student carrels. Some laboratories, however, cannot tolerate natural light.

The roof profile follows the general volumetric outlines of the pitched roofs typically seen on the campus, but is a knife-edged copper translation from the predominant Spanish tile. This winglike, cantilevered eave projection forms a horizontal soffit. The entire roof assembly floats above a nine-inch band of glass which is continuous around the entire perimeter of the building.

Common circulation areas sometimes open to balconies, which are excavations into the imagined stone block.

The copper-vaulted loggia is part of a sequence that includes the lobby and courtyard beyond—the entire area is available for freely flowing events and receptions.

The internal programmatic requirements suggested a building on four levels, with a combination of wet and dry laboratories, study carrels, faculty offices, an assembly space, and public circulation areas that would link to the courtyard. Mediating and separating the new building from the existing Center, the courtyard is used for receptions and other public functions.

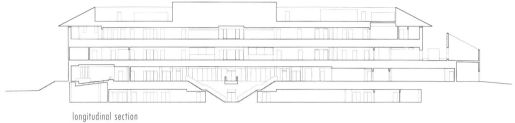

longitudinal section

The glass-covered skeletal overhang, a ghost form of the roof, projects over the courtyard and incised balconies. The glazed end wall of the existing Center reflects the south face of the new building.

The building ends to the west with a concrete vault whose sloping profile projects the line of the copper roof above. This bunkerlike element, set away from the body of

the stone building, stores hazardous gasses used in the laboratories.

center for integrated systems

The Nanoscale Center anchors the
northwest corner of the campus.
When viewed from the air, the forms
of the higher elements of the building
have a generalized relationship to the
existing campus buildings, but the
spiraling inner courtyard is an
exception to the essentially double-
loaded bar building typology that
dominates the campus. Offering a very
different experience, this spiraling,
ascending organization also affords
continual views into the courtyard,
which is the focus of the building.

center for nanoscale science and technology rice university houston texas

The apertures in the skin of the building relate to the function within—the larger, sometimes horizontal, glazing is for laboratories or lecture hall; the smaller rectangular windows are for office spaces.

Access to the building from the campus is through a series of small linked quadrangles—which are tributaries to the main quad— culminating in the courtyard around which the building spirals upward.

The linked quads extend an axial movement to the west, which continues through the building by way of a double set of glass doors. This positions the building as a gateway to the sports fields and any future development that may occur to the west.

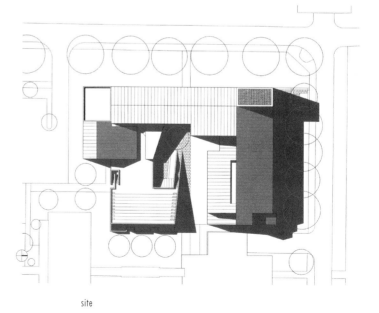

site

The Center relates closely to the existing 1950s Space Sciences building. The courtyard hub, focused on a shade tree,

has access to a second-level roof terrace/bleacher gathering area, which can be used for ceremonies, seminars, and many other events.

Central to the second-level terrace is a copper-clad lounge/reception area. The blackened copper skin distinguishes this crossroad space from the precast concrete and brick perimeter of the body of the building.

The feeling of the building as it spirals around

The spiral configuration of the building is low to the southeast and east and ascends, step by step, to the highest point of the building on the north side. Even in the climate of Houston, it is very important in the winter to have sun penetration into outdoor gathering spaces.

The stepped seating of the terrace bleacher area mirrors the raked floor and stepped ceiling of the lecture hall below.

There are both wet and dry laboratories in the building. Since much of the research equipment is highly sensitive to building vibration, the mechanical equipment for the building is isolated in a subterranean gallery

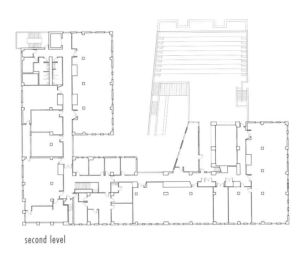

second level

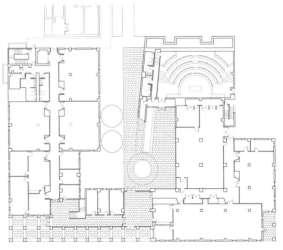

ground level

the courtyard is very different from the street side—the openings are larger and substantial areas of precast concrete are introduced.

At the northwest corner, the tower culminates in a trellised observation deck. The arcade below guides pedestrians into the main entry. The corner tower anchors the northwest corner of both the building and the campus.

In the entry lobby there is a stair enclosed by glass depicting vastly enlarged nanoscale images—almost lost in the nanotube imagery are quarter-inch "nano" portraits of the two Nobel laureates, Rick Smalley and Robert Curl, who are among the users of the Center. The stair is a luminous element that implies the experimental nanoscale realm.

Kaleidoscopic, fractured glass view tubes look into the Nanotechnology

Instrumentation Lab, distorting the instrumentation seen below and implying the inner world of nanoscale science.

The trellised terrace atop the
northwest arrival tower is a social and
instructional gathering place. Views
from the terrace extend over
neighborhoods, campus playing fields,
and fragments of the city skyline.

Dance Facility

The dance facility at UCSD is set in the same eucalyptus grove as the Mandell Weiss Forum/La Jolla Playhouse, but its encounter with the grove embodies a different attitude. With the Mandell Weiss Forum, which fronts a clearing in the grove, the notion was of a mirrored wall that dematerialized the surroundings, a threshold that one moved through to encounter the experience of theater.

The dance facility, on the other hand, is set among the trees. Its organizing, arcing wall is opaque rather than reflective and projects the alignment of the existing mirrored wall of Mandell Weiss.

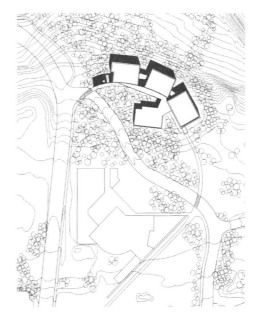

site

Mandell Weiss and the dance
facility each focus on an organizing
wall: one is dematerialized, the
other is solid and creates many
possibilities for dancers.
The dancers can engage openings
in the wall on which choreographic
strategies can be worked. These
same openings allow glimpses into
the grove and the studios
themselves.

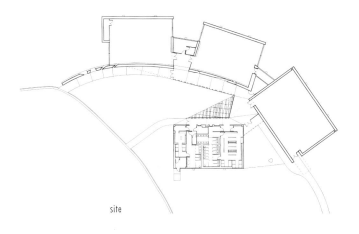

site

The mission of the arcing wall is also to organize the three boxlike dance studios. This building is surrounded by trees at close range with an inner courtyard that is defined by the arcing wall. The mirrored glazing defines circulation, serving the studio and support spaces. All surround this mirror-wrapped courtyard.

The mirror reflects the grove but, relative to Mandell Weiss, is turned inside out—rather than a facade or an outer perimeter, it is an internal lining. The outer perimeter of the dance facility is intentionally opaque and impenetrable, allowing the discovery of the shimmering courtyard within.

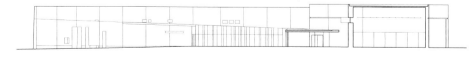

longitudinal section

STUDIO

Seen as a total choreographic venue, all spaces of the building, internal and external, form a linked continuum.

The arcing trajectory of the wall is omnipresent and forms one wall in each of the studios, providing relief from their necessary rectilinearity. Like the inhabitable apertures in the external section of the wall, the gently angled face invites dancers to incorporate the building in their work, rather than treat it as a passive container.

By embracing and including the grove, the choreographic possibility of the site is enormous, with dancers working off the mirror of the inner courtyard. The whole precinct becomes an instrument; and rather than imagining the realm of dance as a formally internalized realm, the building itself enters into possibilities of encounter with the body.

Studio experiences commingle as views connect one studio to the next and to the grove beyond.

The studios are bathed in natural, filtered light because of the close proximity to the eucalyptus grove. The site is very near the bluffs of Torrey Pines, and the soft maritime light of the coast is sometimes filtered through fog and mist, transforming the mirrored condition. These climactic conditions also reinforce the imagery of the studios as a protective huddle amidst the fog.

The black cantilevered canopy projects toward the Mandell Weiss mirror alignment and defines the entrance to the performance studio.

The site is extraordinary in its detachment and solitude amidst this vast landscape—anything built here would be a singular focus.

spencer theater for the performing arts ruidoso new mexico

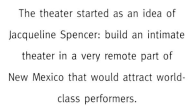

The theater started as an idea of
Jacqueline Spencer: build an intimate
theater in a very remote part of
New Mexico that would attract world-
class performers.

The site is a high alpine meadow
covered with tall native grasses and
piñon and juniper trees. In almost any
direction a mountain range is visible.
Exactly on axis from the site to the
west is the snow-capped, 12,000-foot
peak of Sierra Blanca, which mediates
this high alpine plateau to the lower
elevation of White Sands and
Alamogordo west of the mountains.
The Capitan Ridge forms
a visual wall to the north and ends
in an eroded group of pinnacles
to the east.

From that matrix of land form and
high plain, the Spanish limestone
wedge rises from the earth.

From ten miles away, one sees this apparition sitting on the mesa—pristine and isolated.

The act of absorbing the ninety-foot-high fly loft in the continuous slope of the building was a very important goal for me, and for the client; we didn't want the typical boxlike stage house projecting out of the performance space.

The clay model, larger than I normally make, explored the faceted geometry of both the body of the building and the erupting crystalline lobby.

On the west side of the building, the surface of the wedge is folded diagonally, creating two planes—one sloping, one vertical. An outdoor stage, with adjacent stepped terraces and a grassy area for seating, is carved into the lower vertical plane.

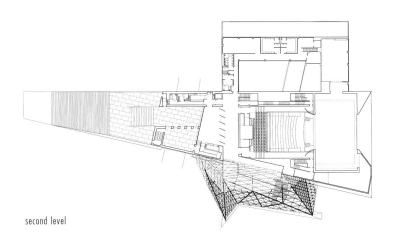

second level

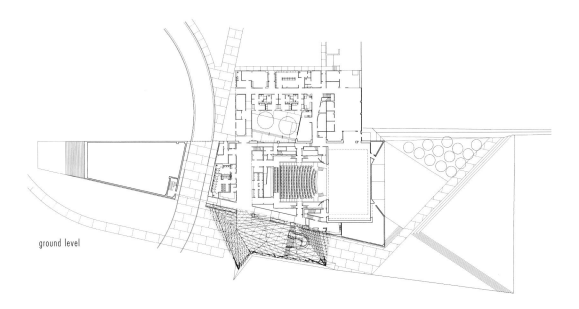

ground level

The faceted lobby, depending on the
light conditions, is opaque and
reflective, or glows from within.
In the winter, when the building and
the landscape merge, the fractal
energy of the lobby becomes the
focus of the building when
encountered at dusk.

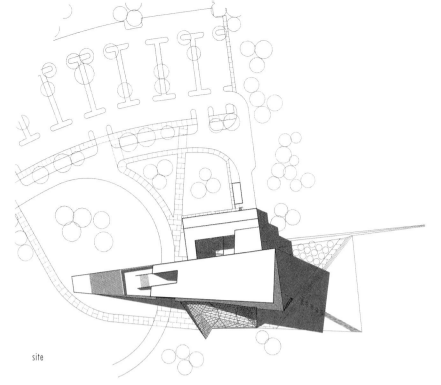

site

The crystalline lobby erupts from the north flank of the building, suggesting a fragment of a Stealth fighter lodged in the side of the stone cliff.

The transverse lobby feeds directly off of the main entry to the theater, and also from an all-weather porte cochere entry point. The lobby links to a patio beyond that is surrounded by back-of-house functions: dressing rooms, green room, and administrative support spaces.

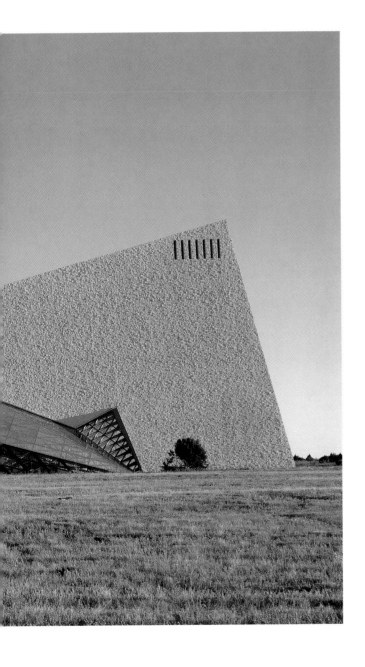

There is an implicit theatricality in the
stepping water-covered surface of the
wedge, the celebratory notched
terrace, and the luminous lobby. Alone
on the high desert plateau, the
building is a welcoming apparition in
the vast landscape. At night, the
building reflects moonlight and
the glow from the lobby, rendering
the entire silhouette a theater
of encounter.

The cascade of water that covers the sixty-eight steps glazes and dematerializes the descending slope of the building.

The lobby, erupting from the angled north wall, sparkles with a thousand halogen fixtures and suggests an inhabited chandelier—an icon of traditional theaters. Ceremony, ritual, procession, and celebration are summed up in the entire experience.

From the lobby, the view alignment escapes to the west, sliding along the edge of the limestone facet on the north side to aim directly at the peak.

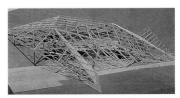

The crystalline imagery of the lobby contrasts the white limestone monolith, a surrogate Sierra Blanca.

The internal volumetric condition of the monolith is suggested by the light that escapes from the excavated apertures in the north flank, which are sheltered by the steel and glass lobby.

Entry into the lobby is via the eastern glass doors. Once inside, one uses the transverse lobby or ascends the glass staircase to the upper lobby. The accumulation of structure and glazing creates a trellislike matrix of shade with fritted glass positioned according to the most critical sun alignments.

Within the lobby are two levels, the main level and an upper lobby that is accessed by the crystalline stair, whose balustrade is rendered in cracked laminated glass, shattering the refracting light in the spirit of the faceted, folded geometries of the lobby.

By containing the fly loft within the continuous profile of the main volume of the building, a large volume was created over the orchestra and balcony seating that gives great acoustical flexibility.

Draperies on tracks, hung in the overhead void, can be deployed from concealed pockets. The curtains are black, lost in the dark void of the upper catwalk lighting zone, and are used to tune the 500-seat space for particular performances—spoken word, music, etc.

A covered dining loggia, an extension
of the upper level theater club,
flanks the terrace with focused views
to the Capitan Ridge to the east.

The building emerges from a still pool. Water issues from the end wall of the eastward-oriented notched terrace and cascades down the steps to rejoin the pool below.

As a white monolith, the roof becomes one of the building facets—its membrane roof, the color exactly matching the stone, alludes to the snow-

capped peak of the white mountain—Sierra Blanca. It is in conscious contrast to the summer earth colors of the high plateau.

Project Chronology

Selected Bibliography

1998

Betsky, Aaron. "Antoine Predock pairs enigmatic Forum Theater of the University of California, San Diego with a new Dance Studio," *Architecture*, August 1998, 62–67. *Dance Facility, University of California, San Diego.*

Castle, Helen. *Modernism.* London: Academy Editions, 1998.

Coke, Margaret. "Structures with Soul: Cubist Combinations of Multiple Fractured Images," *The New York Times Magazine*, January 30, 1998. *Las Vegas Children's Museum and Central Library.*

Doth, Laura. "Curtain Rises at Ruidoso's Spencer Theater," *New Mexico Magazine*, January 1998, 34–39.

Forgey, Benjamin. "Downtown, Art & Soul," *Washington Post*, May 2, 1998, C5. *Arizona Science Center.*

Frampton, Kenneth. *Technology, Place, & Architecture: The Jerusalem Seminar in Architecture.* New York: Rizzoli International Publications, 1998. *Fuller House; American Heritage Center, University of Wyoming, Laramie; Nelson Fine Arts Center, Arizona State University; Venice House; Turtle Creek House.*

Henderson, Justin. *Museum Architecture.* Rockport, Mass.: Rockport Publishers, 1998, 6, 134–139, 190. *Arizona Science Center*

Holmes, Ann. "New Home of the Buckyball," *Houston Chronicle*, April 30, 1998, D1 and 4. *Center for Nanoscale Science and Technolgy.*

Raether, Keith. "Antoine Predock Power of Place," *The News Tribune* (Tacoma, WA) April 26, 1998, D1–3. *Tacoma Art Museum.*

———. "Architect Sees His Craft as Form of Devotional Expression," *The News Tribune* (Tacoma, WA), April 26, 1998, D2.

———. "Come Along on Spiritual Journey to Art Museum," *The News Tribune* (Tacoma, WA), May 24, 1998. B1. *Tacoma Art Museum.*

Soler, Cristina. *Education and Culture.* Barcelona: Links International, 1998, 108–117. *American Heritage Center, University of Wyoming, Laramie.*

Steele, James. *Architecture Today.* Phaidon Press, 1998, 110, 120–125, 128, 242, 265. *Las Vegas Children's Museum and Central Library; Mandell Weiss Forum; Nelson Fine Arts Center, Arizona State University; Venice House; Zuber Residence.*

Stein, Karen D. "The Dramatic Forms of Antoine Predock's Spencer Theater Are Drawn from the Natural Elements on its Isolated Southwestern Site," *Architectural Record*, May 1998, cover, 152–159.

Truppin, Andrea. "Viewers Become Participants in New Predock Museum at Skidmore College," *Architectural Record*, April 1998, 42.

Updike, Robin. "Architect seeks soul of the Northwest," *The Seattle Times*, May 22, 1998, F5.

Zaballebeascoa, Anatxu, ed. *Antoine Predock: Architecture of the Land.* Barcelona: Gustaro Gili, 1998.

1997

Baker, Geoffrey. *Antoine Predock, Architectural Monograph No. 49.* London: Academy Editions, 1997.

Bennett, David. "New Mexico Arts Center Impresses Jazz Legend," *El Paso Times*, October 4, 1997, B1. *Spencer Theater.*

Betsky, Aaron, ed. *Icons: Magnets of Meaning.* San Francisco: Chronicle Books, 1997, 236, 238, 240, 242–243. *Nelson Fine Arts Center, Arizona State University; Atlantis Hotel and Casino.*

Chow, Phoebe. "Stanford Systems," *The Architectural Review*, November 1997, 50–53. *Center for Integrated Systems, Stanford University.*

Cramer, Ned. "On the Boards," *Architecture*, November 1997, 59. *Gateway Center, University of Minnesota.*

Davey, Peter. "America Rediscovered," *The Architectural Review*, November 1997, 4–5. *Center for Integrated Systems, Stanford University.*

Dillon, David. "Playing the Competitions Game," *Architectural Record*, November 1997, 62–67. *Danish National Archive; Atlantis Hotel and Casino; Nelson Fine Arts Center, Arizona State University.*

Dixon, John Morris. "Due Recognition," *Harvard Design Magazine*, Summer 1997, 54. *La Luz Community.*

Doubilet, Susan, and Daralica Boles. *American House Now: Contemporary Architectural Directions.* New York: Universe Publishing, 1997, 13, 110–120. *Fuller House.*

Fuji, Wayne, and Yukio Futagawa. "Antoine Predock," *GA Document 52*, 1997, 21–29. *Arizona Science Center.*

"The Gateway is Under Way," *Minnesota Magazine*, November/December, 1997, 14–18.

Gibson, Daniel. "Shrine to the Arts," *The Denver Post*, October 5, 1997, 12, 13, 22–23. *Spencer Theater.*

Gregory, Daniel. "Nature Gallery," *Sunset Magazine*, October 1997, 108. *Turtle Creek House.*

Guilfoil, Michael. "The Spirit of a Place," *The Spokesman Review* (Spokane, WA), August 5, 1997, D1 and D8. *American Heritage Center, University of Wyoming, Laramie; Arizona Science Center; Nelson Fine Arts Center, Arizona State University.*

Hertelendy, Paul. "Recital Hall is Music to Region's Ears," *San Jose Mercury News*, February 1, 1997. *Music School, University of California, Santa Cruz.*

Hess, Alan. "UCSC Hills Are Alive with the Sound of Music," *San Jose Mercury News*, January 12, 1997, 1C and 3C. *Music School, University of California, Santa Cruz.*

Hill, David. "For New Campus Buildings, Colorado College Reaches for Stars," *Architectural Record*, December 1997, 33.

International Architecture Yearbook No. 4. Victoria, Australia: Images, 1997, 166–167, 188–89, 194–95, 392. *Center for Integrated Systems, Stanford University; Music School, University of California, Santa Cruz; Arizona Science Center.*

International Architecture Yearbook No. 3. Victoria, Australia: Images, 1997, 128–129, 222– 223, 226–227, 310–421. *Ventana Vista Elementary School; Mesa Library; Museum of Science and Industry.*

Jodidio, Philip. *New Forms—Architecture in the 1990s.* Cologne: Taschen, 1997, 105– 107, 126–231. *American Heritage Center, University of Wyoming, Laramie.*

Kai-sun, Katherine. "Predock Builds Dance Studio in Forest of Eucalyptus Trees," *Architectural Record*, January 1997. *Dance Facility, University of California, San Diego.*

Knox, Barbara. "From the Desert to the Prairie," *Minnesota Magazine*, May/June 1997, 52–56. *Gateway Center, University of Minnesota.*

Kruit, Caroline. "Architectonische expressie door constructieve vormgeving," *Architectuur & Bouwen*, October 1997, 3, 12–13.
American Heritage Center, University of Wyoming, Laramie; Museum of Science and Industry.

————. "Synergy of Form and Structure Symposium," *Architectuur + Bouwen*, December 1997, 14–15.

Loomis, John. *Dictonnaire de l'Architecture Moderne et Contemporaine*. Paris: Editions, 1997, 728–729.
Nelson Fine Arts Center, Arizona State University; American Heritage Center, University of Wyoming, Laramie.

Mack, Linda. "Ground Breaking is Today for Eye-Catching 'U' Gateway Building," *Star Tribune* (Minneapolis), November 7, 1997, B1 and B7.
Gateway Center, University of Minnesota.

"Noteworthy" *Museum News*, April 1997, 20.
Arizona Science Center.

Pendergast, Sara, ed. *Contemporary Designers*. New York: St. James Press, 1997, 682–685.

Predock, Antoine. *One House Series: Turtle Creek House*. New York: The Monacelli Press, 1997.

"Progressive Architecture Awards," *Architecture*, January 1997, 60–99.

"Rigsarkivet-landsarkivet," *Arkitekten #03*, February 1997, 23.
Danish National Archive.

Stein, Karen. "Two California campuses: Two different worlds," *Architectural Record*, August 1997, 66–75.
Music School, University of California, Santa Cruz; Center for Integrated Systems, Stanford University.

Stieber, Shari. "A Time to Learn and a Time to Play," *Phoenix Downtown*, April 1997, 6.
Arizona Science Center.

Strickland, Carol. "Architects Create Pizazz on Campus," *The Christian Science Monitor*, July 21, 1997, 1 and 10–11.
Nelson Fine Arts Center, Arizona State University; American Heritage Center, University of Wyoming, Laramie.

Water Spaces of the World, Volume 1. Victoria, Australia: Images, 1997, 192–193.
Rio Grande Nature Center.

Wilson, Chris. *The Myth of Santa Fe*. Albuquerque: University of New Mexico Press, 1997, 4, 103, 274, 291–92, 298, 300–304.
Beach Apartments; Nelson Fine Arts Center, Arizona State University; La Luz Community.

1996

Cerver, Francisco Asensio. *Architectural Houses 01*. Barcelona: Atrium International, 1996, 98–107.
Venice House.

Connell, Michael. "Recapturing the Pride of Place," *Stanford Today*, September/October 1996, 48–55.
Center for Integrated Systems, Stanford University.

Dunlop, Beth. *Building a Dream: The Art if Disney Architecture*. New York: Abrams, 1996.

Educational Facilities: 1995–1996 Review. Washington D.C.: AIA Press, 1996, cover, 24–27.
Ventana Vista Elementary School.

Filler, Martin. "Surveying a Century," *House Beautiful*, November 1996, 134.
Robinson-Burney Residence.

Fisher, Thomas. "Memory Palace," *Design Quarterly 168*, Boston: MIT Press, Spring 1996.

Ghirardo, Diane. *Architecture After Modernism*. London: Thames and Hudson, 1996, cover, 79–82.
Hotel Santa Fe, EuroDisney; Las Vegas Library and Children's Museum; Nelson Fine Arts Center, Arizona State University; Winandy Residence.

Hess, Alan. *Hyperwest: American Residential Architecture on the Edge*. New York: Whitney Library of Design, 1996, 54–55, 74–77.
Fuller and Zuber Residences.

————. "Stanford Takes Welcome Turn Toward the Abstract," *San Jose Mercury News*, May 5, 1996. 1F and 3F
Center for Integrated Systems, Stanford University.

Jodidio, Philip. *Contemporary American Architects, Volume II*. Cologne: Taschen, 1996, 128–141.
Thousand Oaks Civic Arts Plaza; American Heritage Center, University of Wyoming, Laramie; Ventana Vista Elementary School.

"Learning in Las Vegas," *Design Quarterly 168*, Spring 1996, 6–19.
Las Vegas Library and Children's Museum.

LeBlanc, Sydney. *Whitney Guide to 20th Century American Architecture: A Traveler's Guide to 220 Key Buildings*. New York: Watson-Gupthill, 1996, cover, 191, 195, 197.
Nelson Fine Arts Center, Arizona State University; Las Vegas Library and Children's Museum; Venice House.

Lopez, Margot. "El espiritu del lugar," *Ta Lingo*, 1996, 16–21.

Mack, Linda. "Antoine Predock chosen to Design "U" Center," *Star Tribune* (Minneapolis), September 15, 1996.
Gateway Center, University of Minnesota.

Moller, Henrik Sten. "Tysk Bunke bryllup," *Politiken*, December 9, 1996.
Danish National Archive.

Myerson, Jeremy, and Jennifer Hudson. *New Public Architecture*. London: L. King, 1996, 110–113.
Thousand Oaks Civic Arts Plaza.

Oldenburg, Ann. "Do You Like This Building?", *USA Today*, June 24, 1996, 1D–2D.

Pagnelli, Carlo. "In the Environment," *L'Arca*, April 1996, 16–23.
Museum of Science and Industry.

Pearson, Clifford A., ed. *Modern American Houses*. New York: Harry N. Abrams, 116–119, 142–143.
La Luz Community.

"Reflections on Maison de Verre," *Neo: A Journal of Innovation and Rediscovery*, Fall 1996, vol. 5, 17.

Seal, Margaret. "Community Spirit," *The Architectural Review*, February 1996, 64–69.
Thousand Oaks Civic Arts Center.

Toy, Maggie. "Colour in Architecture," *Architectural Design*, April 1996, cover, 64–71.
Museum of Science and Industry.

Wagner, Michael. "Housing Harmony," *Metropolis*, October 1996, 79.
American Heritage Center, University of Wyoming, Laramie.

Webster, Guy. "The Fun's in the Fin," *The Arizona Republic*, September 18, 1996, 4.
Arizona Science Center.

1995

581 Architects in the World, Japan: Gallery MA, 1995, 377.

"The AD 100 Designers and Architects," *Architectural Digest*, September 1995, 112.
Turtle Creek House.

Bierman, Lindsay. "Freeway Acropolis," *Architecture*. March 1995, 84–93.
Thousand Oaks Civic Arts Plaza.

Castellano, Aldo. "Un borgo civico in California," *L'Arca*, October 1995, 24–31.
Thousand Oaks Civic Arts Plaza.

"Civic Arts Plaza in Thousand Oaks California," *Architektur + Wettbewerbe*, September 1995, 18–19.

Cook, Jeffrey. "Making Place," *Phoenix Home & Garden*, December 1995, 28–32.
Arizona Science Center.

DellaFlora, Anthony. "Celebrity Architect Gets Triple Whammy," *Albuquerque Journal*, April 2, 1995, D12.

"Dialogo Con la Naturaleza," *B.A. La Nacion-Architectura*, June 21, 1995.

Dietsch, Deborah. "Predock's Example," *Architecture*. March 1995, 15.

Dillon, David. "American Visionary," *Architecture*, March 1995, 55–93.

———. "Reading Circle," *Architecture*. March 1995, 68–73.
Mesa Public Library.

Frampton, Kenneth, and David Larkin. *American Masterworks: The 20th Century House*. New York: Rizzoli International Publications, 1995, 272–281.
Fuller Residence.

Fuchigami, Masayuki. "Contemporary Architects—Ideas and Works," *Cross Currents*, 1995, 170–173.

Giovannini, Joseph. "Planting Knowledge," *Architecture*, March 1995, 74–83.
Social Sciences and Humanities Building, University of California, Davis.

Goldberger, Paul. "Architecture: Antoine Predock—Variations on a Cube in Southern California," *Architectural Digest*, March 1995, 110–119.
Turtle Creek House.

———. "Houses as Art," *The New York Times Magazine*, March 12, 1995, 46–47.
Rosenthal House.

Gorman, Jean. "Best in Residential Design," *Interiors Magazine*, January 1995, 102–103.
Turtle Creek House.

———. *Detailing Light*. New York: Whitney Library of Design, 1995, 198–201.
Nelson Fine Arts Center, Arizona State University; Thousand Oaks Civic Arts Plaza.

Hammond, Sara. "School is a Beautiful Place to Learn," *Arizona Daily Star*, March 22, 1995, 3B.
Ventana Vista Elementary School.

International Architecture Yearbook, June 1995, 152–155.
American Heritage Center, University of Wyoming, Laramie.

Ivace, Fulvio. "A. Predock a Laramie Wyoming," *Abitare*, February 1995, 138–141.
American Heritage Center, University of Wyoming, Laramie.

Kroloff, Reed. "Sculptural Sequence," *Architecture*, November 1995, 84–93.
Museum of Science and Industry.

———. "Desert Education," *Architecture*, March 1995, 58–67.
Ventana Vista Elementary School.

Lundin, Diana E. "Starry, Starry Nights," *L.A. Life*, July 13, 1995, 12–13.
Thousand Oaks Civic Arts Plaza.

Montaner, Josep M. *Museums for the New Century*. New York: Rizzoli, 1995, 178–183.
Las Vegas Library and Children's Museum.

Ojeda, Oscar Riera. *The New American House*. New York: Whitney Library of Design, 1995, 88–95.
Turtle Creek House.

"Playing the Angles," *Los Angeles Times*, January 8, 1995.

Predock, Antoine. *Antoine Predock*. Seoul: Korean Architects, 1997.

Predock, Antoine. *Architectural Journeys*. New York: Rizzoli International Publications, 1995.

Sicuso, Francisco. "A. Predock y sus Juegos Geometricos," *La Prensa*, March 6, 1995, 6.
Rosenthal House.

Stocker, Lori. "A Square It's Not," *World Architecture*, July 1995, 94–97.
Thousand Oaks Civic Arts Plaza.

"Trails of the Imagination, Part II," *New Mexico Designer/Builder Magazine*, July 1995, 5–11.

"Trails of the Imagination," *New Mexico Designer/Builder Magazine*, June 1995, 6–10.

Tzonis, Alexander; Liane Lefaivre; and Richard Diamond. *Architecture in North America Since 1960*. New York, Bulfinch Press, 1995, 200–203.
Rio Grande Nature Center; Las Vegas Library and Children's Museum.

Von Lessing, Lukas. "Die Visioneneiner Wustenratte," *ADAC Special*, October 1995, 26–32.
Rio Grande Nature Center; Las Vegas Library and Children's Museum.

Welsh, John. *Modern House*. London: Phaidon Press, 1995, 48–55.
Zuber House.

Whiteson, Leon. "Through the looking glass," *Architecture*, March 1995, 125–129.
Rosenthal House.

1994

"A new home for the books," *Los Alamos Monitor*, October 9, 1994.
Mesa Public Library.

"Architecture, History and Memory" in *The Jerusalem Seminar in Architecture*, Jerusalem: Yad Hanadiv, November 1994, 28–31.

Architecture Now 5. Japan: Sigma Union Inc., 1994, 5-1 to 5-12.
CLA Cal Poly.

Armando, Diego R. "Antoine Predock y el Teatro Mandel Weiss," *Consejo Profesional de Arquitectura y Urbanismo*, July 1994, 48–52.
Mandell Weiss Forum.

Bartolucci, Marisa. "Power," *Metropolis*, December 1994, 64–65.
Hotel Santa Fe.

Betsky, Aaron. "Latin Lessons," *Metropolis*, November 1994, 62–63.
Nelson Fine Arts Center, Arizona State University.

Collins, Brad, and Juliette Robbins, eds. *Antoine Predock Architect*. New York: Rizzoli International Publications, 1994.

"Curtain Up," *Los Angeles Times*, October 16, 1994.
Thousand Oaks Civic Arts Plaza.

"Geografia Cultural," *Arquitectura Viva*, September/October 1994, 46–49.
American Heritage Center, University of Wyoming, Laramie.

Graaf, Vera. "Atlantis in der Neuen Welt," *Architektur & Wohen*, December 1994/January 1995, 101–109.
Las Vegas Library and Children's Museum; Atlantis Hotel and Casino.

Kegel. "Zentrum fur das Amerikanische," *Architektur Innenarchitektur Technischer Ausbau*, July 8, 1994, 15.
American Heritage Center, University of Wyoming, Laramie.

Predock, Antoine. "New Visions for Old Age—Airstream Nomads," *Architecture*, October 1994, 90.

Steele, James, ed. *Museum Builders*. London: Academy Editions, 1994, 192–201.
American Heritage Center, University of Wyoming, Laramie; Las Vegas Library and Children's Museum; Nelson Fine Arts Center, Arizona State University.

Webb, Michael. *Architects' Guide to Los Angeles*. San Francisco: The Understanding Business, 1994.
Venice House.

Selected Awards

1998

Award
Concrete, Reinforced Steel Institute
Design Awards XIV
Arizona Science Center
Phoenix, Arizona

Merit Award
AIA & *Sunset* Magazine
Turtle Creek House
Dallas, Texas

Honor Award
Western Mountain Region AIA
Spencer Theater
Ruidoso, New Mexico

1997

Outstanding Concrete Project
Southwest Contractor Best of 1997
Arizona Science Center
Phoenix, Arizona

Merit Award
Arizona AIA
Arizona Science Center
Phoenix, Arizona

Honor Award
New Mexico AIA
Arizona Science Center
Phoenix, Arizona

Merit Award
New Mexico AIA
Student Affairs and Administrative
Services Building
University of California, Santa Barbara

Merit Award
Western Mountain Region AIA
Arizona Science Center
Phoenix, Arizona

Merit Award
Western Mountain Region AIA
Center for Integrated Systems
Stanford University, Stanford, California

Merit Award
AIA California
Center for Integrated Systems
Stanford University, Stanford, California

Merit Award
Western Mountain Region AIA
Mesa Public Library
Los Alamos, New Mexico

Merit Award
Western Mountain Region AIA
Music Center
University of California, Santa Cruz

Merit Award
United States Institute for
Theater Technology, Inc.
Civic Arts Plaza and Performing Arts Center
Thousand Oaks, California

1996

Honorable Mention
New Mexico AIA
Center for Integrated Systems
Stanford University, Stanford, California

Honor Award
Western Mountain Region AIA
Turtle Creek House
Dallas, Texas

Honorable Mention
New Mexico AIA
Museum of Science and Industry
Tampa, Florida

Merit Award
Los Angeles AIA,
NEXT LA Design Awards
Atlantis Hotel and Casino
Las Vegas, Nevada

Merit Award
California Council AIA
Civic Arts Plaza and Performing Arts Center
Thousand Oaks, California

Award of Excellence
AIA/National Concrete Masonry Association
Mesa Public Library
Los Alamos, New Mexico

Special Merit Award of Excellence
AIA/National Concrete Masonry Association
Ventana Vista Elementary School
Tucson, Arizona

Winner, 1996 Best Buildings
New Mexico Business Journal, New Mexico
Associated General Contractors
Mesa Public Library
Los Alamos, New Mexico

Design Award
Concrete Reinforced Steel Institute,
Design Awards XIII
Social Sciences and Humanities Building
University of California, Davis

Honor Award
Los Angeles AIA
Civic Arts Plaza and Performing Arts Center
Thousand Oaks, California

Honorable Mention Award
Western Mountain Region AIA
Civic Arts Plaza and Performing Arts Center
Thousand Oaks, California

Exhibitions

"Eight on the Edge: New Architecture in the West," University Art Gallery,
University of California, San Diego, 1998.

"Building Culture Downtown: New Ways of Revitalizing the American City,"
National Building Museum, Washington, DC, 1998–1999.

"Icons: Magnets of Meaning,"
San Francisco Museum Of Modern Art, 1997.

5-1-6 University Art Museum Downtown,
Albuquerque, New Mexico, 1996.

Disney Biennale Exhibit, Venice, Italy, 1996.

Massachusetts Institute of Technology,
Cambridge, Massachusetts, 1995.